HATFIELD
AND ITS PEOPLE

THE STORY OF A NEW TOWN, A GARDEN CITY,
AN OLD VILLAGE, A HISTORIC HOUSE, THE
FARMS AND THE COUNTRYSIDE
IN A HERTFORDSHIRE PARISH

discovered and related by
the
HATFIELD W.E.A.

(Members of the Hatfield Local History Tutorial Class of
Cambridge University Extra-Mural Board, organized by the
Hatfield Branch of the Workers' Educational Association, under
the tutorship of
Lionel M. Munby, M.A.)

PART 6

LAW AND DISORDER

First published, April 1961
Published with index, April 2014

First published by the Hatfield Branch of the
Workers' Educational Association 1961

Published with index by Hatfield Local History Society 2014

Printed on demand via www.lulu.com

Original text by Nancy Brown
Line drawings by Angela Brown
Photographs from various sources
Index by Hazel K. Bell
Cover design by Henry W. Gray

This reprint was prepared by members of Hatfield Local History Society
with the kind permission of the Workers' Educational Association.

ISBN 978-0-9928415-5-3

COVER DESIGN

Top: Hatfield police, circa 1880

Bottom: County Police Headquarters, St. Albans Road, circa 1960

HERTFORDSHIRE CONSTABULARY
CADET CORPS

THE HERTFORDSHIRE CONSTABULARY CADET CORPS exists to prepare suitable boys for a career in the Police Force.

A comprehensive programme of training is followed, and among the subjects taught are judo, boxing, wrestling, swimming, radio procedure, vehicle maintenance and elementary police duties. Uniform is provided free of charge.

Cadets are employed at various police stations throughout the County—generally at the one nearest to their homes—and they serve periods of attachments to the C.I.D., Traffic Department, Administration Branch, and other sections of the Force.

They are released from duty to attend Colleges of Further Education where they take G.C.E. Courses at "O" and "A" Levels, and allowances are paid to those studying at evening classes.

Hertfordshire Cadets take part in the Duke of Edinburgh's Award Scheme, and attend "Outward Bound" Courses, as well as special residential courses arranged from time to time within the Force.

PAY

At 16 years the commencing pay is £21 13s. monthly, rising by normal increments to £26 13s. at 18 years, but higher rates are paid to cadets who possess the G.C.E. "O" Level in English and two other subjects.

On appointment to constable at 19 years the pay is £50 monthly.

QUALIFICATIONS

    (a) Age between 16 and 17 years.
    (b) British by birth and parentage.
    (c) Not less than 5 ft. 8 ins. tall (without shoes).
    (d) Have good physique, health, eyesight and colour vision.

HOW TO APPLY

Boys who are interested in a sound career with prospects and security should write without obligation for further details to:

THE CHIEF CONSTABLE,
CADET RECRUITING DEPARTMENT,
POLICE HEADQUARTERS,
HATFIELD, HERTS.

FOREWORD

WHEN this series of booklets was published 50 years ago, it was rightly regarded as an exceptionally authoritative and informative work. It has since remained unchallenged as the prime source of reference for anyone interested in the history of Hatfield. Recognising its enduring value, members of Hatfield Local History Society have undertaken this reissue.

Since the booklets first appeared, some of the information contained in them has inevitably become out of date. Hatfield has been affected by sweeping changes, not least by the departure of the aircraft industry and the establishment in its place of a flourishing university and business park. Nevertheless, the original series has stood the test of time remarkably well. We know from our own research experience that it remains immensely useful and we have decided against attempting any piecemeal revision. Instead we have thought it better to reproduce the original booklets without making any changes, except for correcting obviously unintended typographical errors. An important difference is that much more comprehensive indexes have been added.

We hope that the reappearance of the work will stimulate others to undertake new research into Hatfield's more recent past.

Amongst the team who have undertaken the reissue is Henry W. Gray, M.V.O., one of the authors who took part in the W.E.A. class, led by the late Lionel Munby, which produced the original series. The others are Christine Martindale and Jane Teather, Chairman and Publications Officer respectively of Hatfield Local History Society, Hazel K. Bell, who created the new comprehensive indexes, Robin Harcourt Williams, formerly Librarian and Archivist to the Marquess of Salisbury, and G. Philip Marris who led the project.

Thanks are due to Mill Green Museum for allowing some of the original photographs to be re-scanned.

The *Workers' Educational Association,* founded in 1903, is a charity and the UK's largest voluntary sector provider of adult education, delivering 9,500 part-time courses for over 74,000 people each year in England and Scotland.

Hatfield Local History Society is an association of people interested in the history of Hatfield. The Society's aims and objectives are to encourage and undertake research into Hatfield's history, to produce publications and to provide a forum for the exchange of information on the history of the Hatfield area.

The Society is grateful to the copyright owners, the Hatfield Branch of the Workers' Educational Association, for permission to reissue the *Hatfield and its People* series. The complete list of titles is as follows:

Part 1   A Thousand Years of History
Part 2   The Story of Roe Green and South Hatfield
Part 3   Pubs and Publicans
Part 4   Newgate Street
Part 5   Roads and Railways
Part 6   Law and Disorder
Part 7   Churches
Part 8   Schools
Part 9   Farming Yesterday and Today
Part 10   Houses
Part 11A   Families and Trades (Part A)
Part 11B   Families and Trades (Part B)
Part 12   The Twentieth Century.

Please contact Hatfield Local History Society for further information about this publication.

INTRODUCTION

THESE booklets represent the work over a number of years of a group of Hatfield inhabitants in a tutorial class run by the Hatfield Branch of the Workers' Educational Association under the tuition of Lionel Munby, M.A., Staff Tutor of the Extra Mural Board of Cambridge University. They are : Mrs. G. M. Brown, Mrs. N. Brown, Mr. S. H. Dawson, Mr. W. H. Dunwoodie, Mr. H. W. Gray, Mrs. B. Hutton, Dr. K. Hutton, Mrs. M. Malcolm, Mr. W. Malcolm, Mr. T. L. Padget, Mr. M. A. Pinhorn, Mr. J. A. Preston, Mr. D. H. Spence.

For this booklet the following sources have been consulted:

i   Court Rolls of Hatfield Manor.

ii   Hatfield Manor Papers transcribed by R. T. Gunton,
      both in the archives of Hatfield House.

iii "Life on the English Manor", H. S. Bennett.

iv Sessions Books, published by the County Record Office, Hertford.

v   "Local Government in England and Wales", W. Eric Jackson.

vi "Principles of Local Government Law", W. Ivor Jennings.

vii "The Police of Herts", article by Claude Hamilton in the Hertfordshire Countryside, Spring 1958.

viii Account and minute book of the Hatfield Association for the Prosecution of Felons, County Record Office.

ix Files of the various county newspapers, County Record Office.

x   "Police", John Coatman.

xi "Some Memories of Bishops Hatfield", Rev. J. J. Antrobus.

We would also like to thank the following: The County Archivist, Col. le Hardy, and his staff for constant willing help; Lord Salisbury for access to archives and for permission to reproduce Fig. 1; the Chief Constable, A. F. Wilcox, Esq., and Inspector R. H. Oliver for much help and permission to reproduce Figs. 6 and 7; the Librarian of Hatfield Technical College; Mr. W. Branch Johnson; Miss Angela Brown for Figs. 2 and 3; Mr. Henry Gray for the cover design and Mr. Lionel Munby for all his help and advice. We regret that Mr. S. H. Dawson, who did some of the earliest work on this subject and whose help would have been so useful in later stages, left the district before the time came for writing it up.

Published by the Hatfield Branch of the Workers' Educational Association

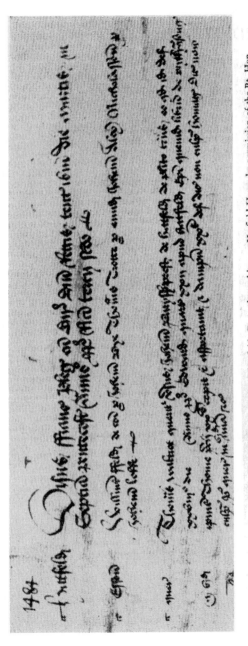

Fig. 1. The opening lines of an early court roll of Hatfield. From the archives at Hatfield House by permission of the Rt. Hon. The Marquess of Salisbury.

[*Photo: Basil King*]

	LATIN		ENGLISH
1484 Hattfield.	Visus ffranc plegii cum Cur(ia) Dom(ini) Regis tent' ib(ide)m Die martiis in Septia pentecost Anno r(egni)r(egis) Ric(ar)di tercii sec(undo).	1484 Hatfield.	View of Francpledge and court of our Lord the King held this Tuesday in the week preceding Whitsun in the second year of the reign of King Richard III.
Esson(iati).	William ffelde de co(mmun)i per Joh(ann)em Pye, Thomas Trotte per eund(em) Joh(ann)em, Alex(ander) Nicholasson per Joh(ann)em Lokke.	Essoins.	William Field sends his excuses from ordinary court business by John Pye, Thomas Trotte by the same John, Alexander Nicholasson by John Lokke.
quer(entes).	Thomas Waltrot querit versus Johannem paryshprest de hattfeld de placito eius eo quod id def. XXVIII die —anno r(egni)r(egis) Edwardi quarti XXII apud hattfeld ep(iscop)i quemd(am) Libr(um) de prykkyngsong ipsuis Thomc pr(ec)ii XX s. cepit et apportavit, et dampnum XX s. Def. dic. non culp., hommage dic. non culp., ideo quer. in merc. 6d. etc.	Pleas.	Thomas Waltrot complains against John the parish priest of Hatfield concerning his (earlier) plea against him that (John) on 28th — in the 22nd year of Edward IV's reign at Bishops Hatfield stole and took away a certain book of prykkyngsong of the said Thomas's worth 20s. and (Thomas was awarded) 20s. damages. The defendant pleaded not guilty, the homage awarded not guilty, therefore the plaintiff was in mercy fined 6d. etc.

Note: "prick-song" or "pricking-song" : any printed or written music, hence also music that is composed as against traditional music.

4

Order in the Manor

THE modern forms of law and order owe some of their features to the ancient structure of local administration set up as far back as Saxon times. In those days before the Norman conquest when most people were engaged in agriculture, there were only simple matters to be dealt with, many of which had to do with land tenure.

There were three administrative authorities—the vill, the hundred, and the county. Men of each vill (town or village) were sworn into groups of ten called "tithings", within which each man bore responsibility for the good behaviour of all the ten. It was compulsory for every male over the age of ten to belong to a tithing, though this did not apply to knights, feudal lords, or clergy. Each tithing group was headed by a "tithing man" or "capital pledge", who was responsible for notifying offences. The Saxon tithing system was incorporated into the manorial system, so that the tithings were responsible to the manor court. The manor court met in several capacities. The Court Baron was concerned with free tenants' affairs, the customary court with those of the villeins or bond tenants. The Court Leet and View of Frankpledge were concerned only with juridical, not administrative matters. In practice, most of these functions were carried out at whatever court happened to be sitting, so that entries relating to free or unfree property, administration and justice are often indiscriminately made in the same roll (see Bennett, p. 199).

In Hatfield lived both tenants of Hatfield manor and tenants of some of the sub-manors. We know that the sub-manor of Symondshide held its own courts from a very early date, because court rolls, which are the official minutes, are to be found in the British Museum dated 1366 onwards. The earliest surviving court rolls of Hatfield manor, in the archives of Hatfield House, date from 1482. The beginning of the roll of Whitsun, 1484, is illustrated in Fig. 1. The rolls are in Latin up till about the seventeenth century. They tell us much of what we know about mediaeval Hatfield.

In 1492 the court roll of Hatfield enters that "John Felde is of age 18 years and not sworn of the tithing—fined 4d." Similarly in 1502 Gerard Harman was fined 4d. because Harman his son and John his apprentice, who were both twelve years old and more, were harboured by the said Gerard and not yet sworn of the King's tithing. Tithing groups were based on the hides as convenient geographical localities (see the map in Book 1, Fig. 12, page 20). In 1487 "Thomas Wright tithing man comes with all his tithing of Bokenhamhide (Bukhamwyk) and reports that William Potter is a man sworn of the tithing and does not attend the court".

The manor court had to enforce regulations about the quality and price of goods sold in the village, such as bread and ale. These regulations were called assizes, and to help enforce the assize of ale the court appointed an ale taster (see Book 3, page 5).

Offences against the various assizes were numberless, but this is not surprising since cases of a similar nature are reported from time to time in the newspapers today. In 1482 the roll records that John Denny, a fisherman, sells at an excessive price—fined 2d. In the same year John James and John Turner were fined 4d. each for making bad quality shoes, and again in 1487 John Jemys (probably the same man) and William Gerard were fined 8d. each for using bad leather to make shoes with leggings and other leather goods. In 1483 Alice Basset was fined 2d. for selling candles of bad weight to the grave damage of the neighbours. In 1487 we find a list of 17 persons, nearly all women, who "broke the assize of ale" that is sold ale of inferior quality, excessive price or short measure, and Agnes Rolfe is fined 2d. for keeping a tippling house and breaking the assize.

The manor court also tried to preserve the amenities of Hatfield, or perhaps create them. In 1502 Gerard Harman (see page 5) was ordered to cleanse his necessary house called a privy so that it should no longer injure William Grey; a time limit was set and one shilling penalty fixed. But in 1505 the Harman privy was still causing trouble—Geoffrey Harman was reported to have a privy injurious to the neighbours, and to throw manure into the common (i.e. public) street. Clemencia Harman, widow, was also accused of throwing manure out into the street, and John Newman was alleged to have enclosed a privy greatly injurious to his neighbours. In the same year a general injunction was made that "no tenant shall throw any kind of carcase into the dell called Batterdell under penalty of 40d.".

One of the primary functions of the manor court was to manage the agricultural life of the community, and in the court rolls we find a number of cases dealing with hedging and ditching and the prevention of private encroachment on the common rights. In 1483 we read that "William Pegen has a ditch not cleansed between Auncells and Pegeons for a space of 12 perches, to be amended before the next court under penalty of 12d.". The Lord of the Manor himself was not immune from this kind of supervision, as there are entries about uncleared ditches belonging to him. Other obstructions were dealt with similarly. "Philip Mery has branches of trees growing in the lane called Ded Lane for the space of 16 perches. Ordered to be amended before Michelmas under penalty of 40d.".

Even more serious was the protection of crops growing in the un-hedged open fields. There were many animals loose in the parish to find what grazing they could, and the "wild" beasts in the Lord's Park had to be kept in. In 1482 the court noted that "John Fysshe does not repair the Lord's pales towards the Great Park at Potwellgrove, containing 42 roods, and is ordered to repair the same before Easter under a penalty of 40d.". John is fined because he has not repaired the palings and has had several warnings. "William Feld has badly repaired the Lord's pales towards the Great Park at Bowstyle containing 40 roods." Straying animals could cause a lot of damage in an open-field farming community, so the manor court appointed an official called the pinder, to catch and impound them in the village pound or pinfold. There was a pound at Woodside in 1603; it is shown on the map in Book 1, page 13, as a small square up against the boundary of the Great Wood, below the words "Woodside Place". In the nineteenth century there was a pound opposite the Red Lion. In 1482 the court roll records : "seven stray sheep that have come into the manor are to be proclaimed by the bailiff as strays". "Thomas Waltrot broke the pinfold of the Lord Bishop (of Ely) and took away a bull impounded there, without permission—fined 6d." An example of the damage that could be caused by animals comes in the court roll of 1543 : "John Page must remove the dangerous swine that are accustomed to tear the lambs in pieces, under a penalty of 6s. 8d. No-one may loose his swine on the common of the Town of Hatfield unless ringed, under a penalty of 4d."

The Manor Court also dealt with crimes of violence. In 1483 Thomas Trott (see Fig. 1) and Robert Nelseam, millers, were fined for assaulting Richard Pygges with a "daggario", and drawing blood. On March 20th, 1483, "Nicholas Hyll threw a 'pleynstaff' at one of his horses at plough and the staff returned and struck Johanna Hyll his daughter by mis-fortune upon the head, through which Johanna afterwards died." There is no indication that the court did other than note this tragedy. Cases of immorality and theft also appear in the court records. In 1483 Johanna Downe is reported to the court as a common scold or scandal monger, to the great danger of her neighbours, and is ordered to amend her ways. By the next year the neighbours have had enough of her and the jury says "that Joan Downe is a common thief and strumpet to the common injury of all the neighbours. Therefore she is ordered to quit the town before the feast of the Nativity of St. John the Baptist (mid-summer) under penalty of standing in the pillory."

One of the more unusual thefts is that recorded in the Whitsun court roll of 1484 (see Fig. 1). Thomas Waltrot has accused the parson of stealing his song-book, but the court found that the parson was not guilty and fined Thomas 6d. for bringing a false charge against him. How did Thomas come to have a song-book, one wonders, since it is clear he was not a cleric but a farmer, and his name is commemorated in Waltraps Farm (Book 2, p. 7). Was he perhaps the parish clerk, who had to lead the singing in church?

Various punishments, other than fines, were available to the manor court. The stocks, pillory, whipping post, cage, and a ducking stool for scolds were regarded as the necessary pieces of corrective equipment of every town or village (see Figs. 2 and 3). A cage at one time stood at the

Fig. 2. A Pillory.

bottom of Church Street, for it is marked on a map of 1838. While Elizabeth I was at Hatfield in 1558 we read that "Elizabeth Walshe sat in the stocks in the church yard at Hatfield from six of the clock in the morning until Church time", when she had to make a public confession before the congregation. She was then whipped round the Church walls and redelivered to the stocks until evening prayer. The first House of Correction was established at Bridewell in London in 1555, and others followed throughout the country "for the setting of idle and lewd people to work, and partly for the lodging and harbouring of the poor, sick and weak". We know one was set up in Hatfield in 1598, but not where it was.

The manor court also recorded changes of ownership of property since the incoming tenant had to pay a "fine" to the Lord of the Manor.

8

Fig. 3. Stocks and whipping post as can still be seen at Aldbury (near Tring), Herts.

When his payment was entered in the roll this constituted his title to the land, and he could get a copy of the entry to keep for himself, just as we get a copy of our entries of birth, etc., in the official registers. Thus his land was "copyhold", held by virtue of his copy of the court roll entry. One of the most interesting of this type of entry concerns a very famous Englishman. In 1531 "Sir John More, a Judge of the Common Pleas, surrenders to his son Sir Thomas More, Lord Chancellor of England, a messuage in the Stoke Hyde called Downs . . . and Sir Thomas is admitted" (see Book 2, page 9). In 1546 "Domina Alicia More, widow of Sir Thomas, has died since the last court", her lands fall to the King (Henry VIII) who was at this period Lord of the Manor, "by reason of the attainder of Sir Thomas". Also in 1551, "9s. 5d. yearly rent lately paid out of one farm called Waltrottes is now withdrawn by reason that the farm is in the King's hands by the attainder of the late Sir Thomas More".

Order outside the Manor

Each county was divided into 'hundreds', and Hatfield lies in the Broadwater Hundred of Hertfordshire, named after the original meeting place of the Hundred Court near Stevenage. The Court chiefly dealt with breaches of the peace, where the court of the manor concerned had not acquired the right to handle such cases or where the matter affected more than one manor; but it also had certain duties of a local government nature to perform such as the maintenance of important highways and bridges. Before the Norman conquest the Earl presided over justice in the hundred and shire courts, but this now became the work of the Sheriff. Twice a year the Sheriff attended at the hundred courts to hold his "tourn", that is to judge the more serious cases coming before the court. All free men of the hundred owed suit to (i.e. had to attend) the hundred court, and a man called the hundredor presided for ordinary business, with a jury.

The Sheriffs, who before the Conquest had been less powerful than the Earls, became more and more powerful and oppressive. In 1170 King Henry II conducted an "Inquest on Sheriffs" when their activities were enquired into and many removed from office. Edward II, in 1315, made the office a Crown appointment because too many improperly qualified men were being elected. Nevertheless, in the fourteenth century Sheriffs were very unpopular, and their prestige declined.

Edward III therefore found it necessary from time to time to appoint persons in each county to hear and determine felonies. The first appointment of these "Keepers of the Peace" was in 1327 when Robert de Kendall, Hugh Fitz Simon, and John de Blomvil were commissioned for Hertfordshire. In 1336 Edward III being at Hatfield appointed seven men for Hertfordshire. They were William de Shuneshull (Seneschall?), William Trussel senior, John de Molys, Hugh Fitz Simon, John de Blomvil, Thomas de la Haye, and Roger de Louth. Hugh and Roger (see Book 2, page 8) were leading Hatfield citizens, and probably the others were all local men. From 1350 onwards these men, who came to be called Justices of the Peace, met once a Quarter at Quarter Sessions, and with the aid of the juries of the hundreds tried criminal offences. The Hatfield cases were all heard at the Hertford Quarter Sessions as they are today. The office of Justice of the Peace was formally defined in the statute of 1360; and he carried out duties similar to those of the Sheriffs tourn, taking over more and more of his authority.

In the 1590's there were thirty-five Justices of the Peace within the county of Hertford, among whom we find such familiar Hatfield names as Sir John Brocket, Knight, Sir Philip Boteler, Knight, and Sir Henry Boteler, Esquire.

The Justices in Tudor Times

During the Tudor period, economic changes brought about an increase in the duties of the Justices of the Peace. The wool trade was expanding, and to find grazing for more and more sheep some Lords of the Manor enclosed the arable village fields for sheep-runs. For the first time the number of landless, destitute beggars became a serious problem, which the J.P.'s had to deal with, since the monasteries which had earlier administered relief to the poor had been dissolved. What had formerly been the religious duty of almsgiving now became a secular social problem. In this situation the Elizabethan Poor Law of 1601 was enacted. A compulsory poor rate was levied for the relief of the poor in each parish, and Overseers of the Poor were appointed, responsible to the Justices, to buy material to provide work for the unemployed—"a convenient stock of flax, hemp, wool thread, iron and other stuff to set the poor to work", while for those incapable of work the Overseers provided relief.

A project for setting the poor to work at making cloth was inaugurated in Hatfield in 1608 by Walter and Hugh Morrell under the auspices of the first Earl of Salisbury who provided half a barn, some farm land, and a site for a fulling-mill. Though well intended, the scheme dwindled and died partly because of the antagonism of the miller who complained that his head of water was reduced by the fulling-mill higher up stream, and partly because it could not be made to pay its way. The miller, Rawson, complained against the Morrells in the manor court in 1619, but did not succeed in getting rid of them. In 1628 Rawson invoked another law against the Morrells and had them fined £21 for "taking inmates", i.e. harbouring persons from another parish who might become a charge on Hatfield's poor rate. In 1633 Rawson complained to the Justices.—

1633
That Walter Morrill, of Kings Hatfield, gentleman, diverted a watercourse running between a place called Stanborrowe and a mill in the occupation of Luke Rawson, gentleman, so that the highway is much annoyed.

This story sounds very much like a personal quarrel between Rawson and the Morrells, but it is interesting because it shows a privately sponsored attempt to relieve the poor unemployed on the lines laid down in the 1601 act for the Overseers of the Poor.

It was not the first attempt at poor relief in Hatfield, for in 1607 we read that a house at "Milne Green was built by the inhabitants of Hatfield about thirty years ago for the reception of the poor of the said parish".

Relief for those who could not work was paid by the Overseer and the Churchwardens on the direction of the Justices.

1659
Order that the churchwardens and overseers of Hatfield, shall provide for Jonas Leech.

11

1683
Complaint to the court that Henry and Thomas Slow, two poor children of Hatfield, are in want of relief "they being fatherless, and their mother run away". Order that the churchwardens and overseers shall provide for them.

1698
It is ordered that the overseers of Hatfield shall allow one shilling a week to Thomas Harrington, a poor lame person, who cannot obtain work.

The Act of 1588-9 which prohibited the harbouring of "inmates" or lodgers also provided that no cottage might be built without four acres of freehold land. Although at first sight these two matters might appear to be unconnected, the purpose of the Act was to prevent the immigration of landless peasantry who might become a burden on the parish through their inability to support themselves without land.

1639
Presentment of Thomas Cripps of Hatfield, yeoman, for building a cottage there without laying to the same four acres of land according to the statute.

With the growth of commerce and the increasing population there was a great deal of traffic and roads and bridges were in constant need of repair. Each parish had a Surveyor of Highways whose duty it was to call out the male inhabitants with their horses and tools to do four days' labour on the roads during the year. Stones picked from the fields were thrown into the pot-holes to be flattened by the wheels of passing carts.

1662
Petition of William Catlin and the rest of the surveyors of the highways in the parish of Hatfield to the Justices of the Peace. It states that the highway leading from the north towards London and extending five miles in length through the said parish, is much out of repair, notwithstanding all the inhabitants perform their services in the repair of the roads, but the inhabitants of Newgate Street Ward refuse to do any service under the pretence that they had not formerly any service therein, but in their own private lanes. The petitioners therefore pray that the inhabitants of Newgate Street Ward may be ordered to assist in the repairs of the said great road, as other inhabitants do.

As a number of main roads ran through the county, the maintenance of highways was a matter of considerable importance. The general condition of the roads and bridges was often very bad because of the heavy burdens of the laden carts and waggons passing along them. The Justices sometimes demanded that extra statute work should be done by the inhabitants.

1687
Certificate by two Justices; Recites that the inhabitants of Hatfield were presented for the highway leading from Page's Mill to Hatfield Town, and for a gravel pit near London Road, "digged so near the highway there, and that it was dangerous for travellers", and that Nathaniel Phipp, surveyor of the highways, was also presented for digging a gravel pit in the highway leading from Page's Mill to Hatfield. The two Justices have viewed the said highway, and find it well amended, and have also viewed the said gravel pits, and find that the pit near London Road is sufficiently secured with post and rails, and that near Page's Mill is so far filled up as not to be dangerous to passengers.

Some preferred to pay a fine rather than do the work, and this led in time to the system of levying a money rate.

1650
Upon the petition of the inhabitants of Hatfield, concerning two bridges there near Wildhill, which are out of repair and which ought to be repaired at the charge of the inhabitants, it is ordered that the constables and certain of the said inhabitants shall meet together and make a rate for raising the sum of £5 to be employed about the repairing of the said bridges. Mr. Carter, of Hatfield, is desired by the Bench to see that the said sum is employed as aforesaid.

The business transacted at Quarter Sessions was extremely varied, and besides poor relief and maintenance of highways included criminal cases such as manslaughter, theft and riot, cases of trespass or of bastardy or recusancy (refusal to conform to the established church). The Justices also took over the regulation of trade, price fixing and the licensing of alehouses which had earlier been dealt with in the manor court.

1683
—For selling corn without license:—
William Kilby of Hatfield; Thomas Johnson and Francis Page, Robert Wisman all of Hatfield.

1626
Presentment of Margaret Younge of Hatfield, widow, Henry Tukner, John Abbott, and Henry Smith, all of the same, yeomen, for severally keeping alehouses there, without licence.

1657
Presentment that Thomas Kempster, of Hatfield, victualler, allowed tippling in house during unlawful hours.

1684
Order that Susan Hawkes be suppressed from keeping an alehouse in Hatfield.

Cases of care and protection of apprentices are also recorded. It appears that if a person carried on a trade without having served the normal period of apprenticeship, he could be brought before the Justices—sometimes by paid informers, who received half the fine imposed on the offender!

13th July 1635: Presentment that Richard Sellwood of Hatfield, locksmith, had practised the art or mystery of a linen draper, and without having served an apprenticeship of seven years.

Just as the manor court had tried to stop insanitary practices, so the Justices later received similar complaints and made orders to preserve the amenities of the town.

1649
In July 1649, information was given to the court that John Millard and Samuel Nicholls with others of Hatfield, "do in the very hearte of the towne there, use burning of straw steeped in stale or lye for the making of potashes, the smell of smoake whereof is very noysome and offensive, not only to the inhabitants of the towne, but also to the remote dwellers of that parish, and may by all likelihood prove infectious to the people of the said towne and parish."
Order that the said offence be stopped, or removed to some remoter place.

In January 1650, there was an order that Samuel Nicholls and John Millard, husbandmen, and William Sellwood, tailor, all of Hatfield, shall be bound over in good sureties to appear and answer in the next General Sessions, upon an indictment against them for burning "Straw stepped in uryne or stale, and other filthy waters, to make potashes in the market village near the common highway at Hatfield, whereby the air is made very unwholesome and pestiferous, and the lives of those dwelling near and passing by, are endangered".

An interesting case that the Justices dealt with concerned the licence which had to be obtained before woodland could be turned into tillage. This was no doubt because of the importance of timber for shipbuilding.

1631

Licence granted to Ralph Reddell, plaintiff, to compound and agree with Sir John Spencer, of Offley, defendant, upon information exhibited by the said plaintiff, against the said Sir John, in Easter Sessions last, for cutting and "stocking" up of 90 acres of wood called Whethampstead Springe in the parish of Hatfield, and converting the same into tillage, the said wood having been time out of mind (until the said conversion) been wood, and employed and used for the increase of wood, and being two furlongs distant from the mansion house of the said Sir John to whom the said 90 acres belonged, contrary to the statute in that case, made and provided. The plaintiff is to cause the licence to be entered into the book of orders remaining in the hands of the Custos Rotulorum of this County, or the Clerk of the Peace, and also, before the end of the next General Sessions, shall deliver and set down upon his oath what fine or consideration he had or shall have from the said Sir John, in consideration of composition for the said cause. If the plaintiff does not set down his composition, etc., as aforesaid, then his licence shall be void.

The Poor in the Eighteenth Century

In the later seventeenth century an Act of Settlement (1660) put the treatment of the poor on a different footing. Up till now attempts had been made to find work for the unemployed by providing the materials, and they might build a cottage and settle down where they could get work provided they had the necessary land. Now a poor person had to establish a "settlement" by a year's residence in a parish before becoming eligible for relief, and if such settlement could not be shown he would be sent back to the parish of his birth. This meant that poor persons, beggars, and vagrants were constantly being hustled out of the parish, and sometimes hastened on their way with a whipping. These entries in the Sessions records show vividly the miserable state of vagrants at this time.

1677

Complaint of the parishioners of Hatfield that Anne Thompson, a vagrant, and her child, were sent out of Middlesex to Ludlow, and that she died at Hatfield on her way, leaving her child, aged 9 months, chargeable to the parish. Order that the parishioners of Hatfield shall provide for the child until they can find out where the child was born, or until they can obtain judgement from the Judges of Assizes.

1684

William Wilson, who, with his wife and children was to-day taken as a vagrant, declares that his last settlement was at Hatfield about eight years ago, and that he never had any settlement since, but that he "had wandered and begged abroad" and that he does not know his birthplace. Order that he be sent to the House of Correction and whipped according to law, and that he, his wife and children, be conveyed to Hatfield.

1694

Order that John Jones, his wife and four children, taken at Hatfield as vagrants, be passed to Mold Co. Flint, "in the Dominion of Wales", where he was born. He is given three months to pass.

1699

Charles Cobb, curate, and Henry Blathroe and Michael Hale, churchwardens of Hatfield, signed a pass on the 14th Jan. 1699, stating that Sarah Harrison with a child, who had fallen sick in the parish, had last resided at Cambridge, and had her removed, and desired the officers of Ayott St. Peters and other towns on the way, to conduct her to Cambridge. But Sir Ralph Radcliffe, one of the Justices, wrote on the pass on the 18th February, 1699, that the child has twice been "denied" by the constable of Ashwell to pass to Cambridge, and had the child removed from Hitchin "the next straight way" back to Hatfield, where it was born. Against the latter warrant Hatfield appealed but this appeal was not allowed by the Court.

From 1718 the County appointed a contractor to convey vagrants, and he received £200 for doing this, a sum which remained about the same until in 1784 Mrs. Hunt who had been applying for an advance on salary for several previous quarters, asked for and obtained £10 as extra expenses. The work was clearly becoming too much for a single contractor, and at Michaelmas of the same year three new conveyors of vagrants were appointed for the middle, east and west areas of Herts. One of these was a Hatfield man:

"Joseph Pettitt of Hatfield to have £42 a year for the Hatfield Road, from Barnet, thro' Baldock, Hitchin, or any other place contiguous to the said Road, from the first place in the next jurisdiction northward, and so from those places thro' Barnet or other place to the first place in the next jurisdiction southward, and also from or to any place eastward or westward between the Liberty of St. Albans and the Hertford Road. For conveying and supporting vagrants through the different high Roads of this County."

The following year the Justices laid down in detail their instructions for the greatest possible economy in conveying vagrants.

Another officer who received his expenses from the Justices was the Coroner. In 1827 when Francis James Osbaldeston, of Hatfield, was Coroner he was made an allowance of 9d. a mile "returning as well as going to take Inquisitions". Today, officials of the County Council get a travel allowance of 8d. a mile when on business.

Before the days of insurance, the victims in cases of fire or burglary, could only be compensated by organising a charitable subscription. It was necessary to forward to the Justices a petition and certificate of good behaviour of the petitioners, signed by a person who knew him.

If the Justices approved it, the petition would be passed on to the Privy Council, who might then authorise all parishes in the County to make a collection for the sufferer. The Privy Council's letter was known as a Brief. Here is the record of such a case:

1628
Information to the court that John Packer and Marion Atkins, widow, very poor people of the parish of Hatfield, have fallen into great want by reason of a lamentable fire which burnt down both their dwellings—houses adjoining one another, and destroyed all their goods, etc., and praying for some relief therein. The Justices commend the same to the charitable consideration of the County, and desire the ministers to make collections in their churches, etc., as in like cases has been done.

During the seventeenth century it was customary throughout the county to release prisoners on condition that they joined the colours, as shown by the following example :—

Petition by Richard Bennett, keeper of the House of Correction at Hatfield, showing that Richard Shawe, William Morgan, John Barker and Robert Belcher, were sent to him in March last year (1625) under the hands and seals of the Sheriff of the county, to be kept till they should "be ymploid in forreine service", and that they have remained there ever since, and are all "very sicke" by reason whereof they have been "wonderfulle chargeable" to the said Bennett, not being able to earn anything towards their maintenance. He therefore desires the court to make some order therein. The matter is referred to certain Justices to take some speedy course for their removal.

Criminal Cases

The Justices also dealt with criminal cases. Here are some examples of the various crimes that came up before Quarter Sessions over the years:

Sept. 1st 1635.—Presentment that William Haile of Hatfield, husbandman, at Hatfield assaulted Mary Gates.

24th April, 1634.—That Thomas Marshall of Bishops Hatfield, bricklayer, there assaulted Robert Glover of the same, labourer.

July 14th 1645.—Reginald Payce, committed to gaol for fishing in the several fish ponds of the Earl of Salisbury in Hatfield, and taking and killing "3 Troute of the price of 5 shillings, and picking of 3 pounds of May cherries of the value of 3 shillings",—to remain there for 3 months and until he shall pay the said Earl treble damages "—and shall find sureties for his good behaviour for 7 years, with provision that, if at any time the said Earl shall please to consent to have him discharged, a Justice shall give an order for the same, the said Payce first finding sureties for his good behaviour for one year only.

Two assaults of about this time may be of interest, one, when in 1653, Robert Cecill, Esq., and two gentlemen, all of Hatfield, assaulted Thomas Carpenter; and 12 years later in 1665, when an assault was made on a baker's wife by Henry Cecill, Esq., son of the Hon. Phillip Cecill, Esq. Unfortunately, in neither case is the result recorded.

In 1695 there is a case of bigamy recorded against one, John Dill. The Jury found "Ignoramus" (i.e. We do not know) and discharged him.

In 1704 we find Charles James, James James and Edward Howe, all of Hatfield, indicted for riot, but with no further details given. Then fifty years later, there began a spate of stealing, the objects of larceny appearing to be mainly linen shirts and poultry!

In 1760 we first meet the only Hatfield person—in the records perused—who appeared before the Sessions more than twice. This was Sarah Packer, spinster, who was then indicted for two cases of assault and trespass—no reason given. She was obviously something of a notorious character, although eight years pass before she next appears, in company with John Hughes, labourer, for having a bastard child, and she was ordered to be detained at Hertford Bridewell. In 1771 she was discharged on an indictment for assaulting another woman, and in 1773 she assaulted Francis Smith and this time was sent to prison for three months.

In October 1769 we have the amusing episode of James Harras and the silver spoon, at the Eight Bells. (See Book 3, p. 23).

1777 saw the first record of a new punishment on the receiving end of which were four Hatfield men found guilty of larceny. They were sentenced to work on the Thames for four years, which referred to the prison hulks at Woolwich which were brought into use when transportation to the American colonies ended with the war of 1775.

An interesting case is recorded in 1790 when eleven Hatfield men were indicted for conspiracy. It was some time before the repeal of the Combination Act in 1825 made it legal to belong to a Trade Union, yet that is clearly the sort of union these workmen had formed. Here is the entry :

1790
Indictment of Thomas Arnold, John Corrall, Thos. Peacock, Wm. Maybank, Thos. Nash, John Davies, James Harditch, Wm. Farr, John Wade, Thos. Atkins, Pardoe Green, of Bishops Hatfield, being workmen and journeymen in the art and occupation of papermaking, and employed as such by Thos. Vallance of the said parish, papermaker, for conspiring to compel the said Thos. Vallance to enhance their wages by 1/- weekly, and for threatening that, if he failed to do so, they would quit his service at the expiration of 14 days.
Endorsed: Indictment for a conspiracy.

The paper mill, which lay upstream of the flour mill at Mill Green, was the descendant of the same fulling mill first built by Walter Morrell in 1607. Paper making is mentioned again in 1817.

12th March
Information of Samuel Johnson, of Hatfield, foreman to Thos. Creswick, of Hatfield, papermaker, concerning a theft of rags called knotty rags, Hamburgh rags, and country colours.

Fig. 4. The old paper mill at Mill Green. The present house is modern but stands
on the site of Morrell's, Vallance's and Creswick's mills.

[*Photo: Barbara Hutton*]

In the Hertfordshire County Press of 1826 we read:

Tues., 7th March *Herts Lent Assizes*

Francis Wetherly, David Giddins and Thomas Dickinson were indicted for
burglary on 24-12-25 in the parish of St. Peters at the house of John Smith (Roe
Hide). Trial occupied 9 hours.

Mr. Smith, a tenant of the Marquis of Salisbury, is a farmer. Smith retired
to bed about midnight on Christmas Eve, leaving his wife, son, daughter and
a young man named Dinn in the kitchen playing cards. About 1 a.m. the party
was disturbed by a noise in the passage leading to the kitchen from the outer door.
The kitchen door opened and two men armed with bludgeons with their faces
blackened, appeared. Young Smith stood up and asked what they wanted. The
reply was, "Your money and be cursed to you!". Mrs. Smith went up to one
of them and was struck on head and shoulders by the bludgeons of the men.
Mrs. Smith rushed past the men into the passage to wake her husband and
encountered two more men who knocked her down and bludgeoned her, but she
contrived to crawl to the stairs and call her husband who came down. Meantime
the ruffians had levelled young Smith to the ground, and Dinn also, but upon
hearing the voice of Mr. Smith all the villains beat a hasty retreat, pursued by
young Smith to the gate of a wheatfield not far off. There the 4 men made a
stand and young Smith deemed it prudent to retreat. An alarm was raised and
Wetherly and Giddins were both identified by Mrs. Smith positively. Young
Smith and Dinn were equally certain about Giddins but not so sure about
Wetherly. There were various other corroborating circumstances. Facts not proved
against Dickinson and he was acquitted. Giddins and Wetherly found Guilty
and sentenced to death. They were sent for execution on Wednesday week.

18

Tues., 21st March

Wetherly and Giddins, the 2 men who were left for execution at Hertford Assizes for burglary and outrage at Roe Hide, and who set up an alibi, still strongly assert their innocence and in consequence an inquiry has been instituted and a respite ordered.

Tues., 25th April

Giddins and Wetherly have had their sentences commuted to transportation for life, owing to the kind intervention of the Marquess of Salisbury.

There were many cases of poaching.

19th Jan. 1850.

Poaching—James Hankin, who did not appear, was convicted of snaring a hare on land belonging to the Marquess of Salisbury in the occupation of Mr. Wm. Pickett. Being an old offender, Hankin was convicted in the full penalty of £5, warrant issued for three months imprisonment.

Feb. 2nd. John Ford, of Hatfield, trespassing in search of rabbits on the Marq. of Salisbury's land, fined £2 15s. 6d. including costs, or in default to be remitted to the House of Correction with Hard Labour for two months.

James Pearman, same offence as above, £1 15s. 6d. incl. costs, which was paid.

23rd Feb. 1850. Petty Sessions.

Poaching. David Collins convicted of snaring a rabbit on land of Mr. Church. Defendant, who appeared to be about 16 or 17 years old, said he set the snare because he had nothing to eat. The Bench thought he had been neglected by his parents. Fined 4/6 and 15/- costs, or House of Correction for 14 days.

Three lads named Bracy, Morton and William Collins (brother to last defendant) were convicted of trespassing in search of rabbits in Longfield, Hatfield. Collins, who had previously been convicted for night poaching, was fined 40/- and 11/6 costs or two months in House of Correction. Bracy and Morton 9/- plus 10/- or three weeks each.

The Assizes

From the earliest times the most serious criminal cases were reserved to the King, whose Judges also heard civil actions. An early reference to a civil action is found in 1251: "the nine acres that Adam Crok recovered from the said John Baker in an action before the Itinerant Judges of our Lord the King at Hertford". Here is a criminal case of 1506:

"The (Manor Court) Jury present that John Rogers, formerly of Bishops Hatfield, yeoman, at the feast of Circumcision 20 Henry VII, by force of arms namely a knife, feloniously took and carried away all the chalices of silver and gold to the value of £10, a pyx of silver and gold of the value of 10 marks, and a 'pax' of silver and gold of the value of 10 marks, two candlesticks of silver, parcel gilt, of the value of £5, two cruets of silver and gold of the value of 40 shillings, a censer of silver and parcel of gilt of the value of 13 . . ., a 'nave' (ship) with cover of silver and parcel gilt of the value of 26 shillings and 8 pence, and £3 in money, of the goods and chattels of the Parish Church of Hatfield in the custody of John Billock, John Foster, Thomas Roger and Thomas Astrye, custodians of the goods and ornaments of the said Church, within the view of this court. The case is sent before the King's Justice at the next Assizes to be held in Herts."

The Assizes are still held in Hertford and still deal with the same categories of business.

The Origins of the Police

The word "Constable", now the title of the ordinary policeman, has a long and distinguished history dating back to the Norman Conquest. The Constable was then elected each spring at the Court Leet by his neighbours and served for a year. His duty was to arraign those accused of petty crimes, larcenies, minor assaults or breaches of local regulations, before the Court Leet; which, as has been explained above, was the juridical court of the manor.

By the time we first have records of Hatfield, in the Court Rolls of 1482, there were evidently constables for each district of this large parish. In 1483 William Pegeon and Henry Byrt were elected constables of Bokenhome Hyde. In 1484 John Lokke junior and John Byrt were chosen constables of Lodewikhide in place of John Southwode. The same are chosen constables of the town of Hatfield in place of William Fletcher and John Berne. In 1542 Thomas Dary and Richard Lucas were chosen constables for Hatfield town,—Catmoye for Newgayt Strate and Thomas Brook for "Le Woodsyde". This is the same district as the earlier Bokenham Hide. The constable had not only to report offences but see that penalties were duly exacted and injunctions carried out. In 1538 the court ordered; "the inhabitants and constables are to sufficiently rebuild and repair a pair of Buttes at Batterdell before New Year's Day under a penalty of six shillings and eightpence" Shooting at the butts was encouraged by Royal Proclamations in order to maintain England's supremacy with the long bow and keep up a supply of trained archers for the defence of the country.

In the sixteenth century the manor courts ceased to appoint constables and this duty was often taken over by the parish vestry, who, uncertain if their appointment was fully legal, submitted the constables' names to the Justices for approval. The office was unpaid and generally unpopular especially when the constable's duties were increased owing to the growth of population in the expanding villages and towns.

Up to the time of the Civil War of 1642-9, the parish constable seems to have done a pretty good job within limits, and was generally quite conscientious. The Protectorate from 1653-8 took away the real responsibility for the community disciplining itself through the supervision of its elected members. For many years the people were to all intents and purposes policed by professional troops; the country was divided into ten districts each with a Major General in charge and 30,000 troops were used to enforce law and order. With such a force in readiness it is small wonder that the village constable showed a discreet inefficiency at his job!

After the Restoration in 1660, the ever increasing volume of duties thrust upon the parish constable encouraged the practice of employing deputies, who were often illiterate watchmen or "Charlies", glad of the small pay. After the year 1662, the constable was able to claim from the Justices a fee for the time spent on his duties in addition to reimbursement of actual expenses. In 1704 the Justices order repayment of certain sums to the following petty constables: "Thomas Deere and Thomas Squire of Hatfeild" (sic). In 1711: "order that William Wright, William Hawks, William Pritchard, —. Bartelett, William Kirby and William Coly, late constables of Hatfield, shall be repaid certain sums of money due to them." Later on this became a sort of salary, usually about £3 a year, which is less than unskilled labourers received at the time. It therefore followed that men who offered themselves for employment at such a low rate, might well be considered virtually unemployable.

Crime in the Nineteenth Century

To supplement the constables, in many areas were formed Associations for the apprehension and prosecution of felons. Hatfield was one of these districts, and in the County Record Office at Hertford there is a minute and account book between the years 1807 and 1847 of the "Association of Gentlemen, Farmers, and the Inhabitants of the Parish of Hatfield in the county of Hertford for the Apprehending and Prosecuting felons of all Denominations". The members paid a subscription varying with their rent. This money was used both for giving rewards for information on, or apprehending of, lawbreakers, and also to pay the costs of prosecution.

Thus in 1807 for information on murderers, housebreakers, incendiaries and highway robbers, the Hatfield Association would pay 15 guineas, on horse, sheep, ox, cow or calf stealing, or maiming, 10 guineas, and on breaking palings, hedges or fences, and on wood or turnip stealing, 1 guinea.

Originally the Association met in the One Bell, then kept by William Pallet (See Book 3, p. 14). Later it moved to the Red Lion kept by Charles Beecroft (Book 3, p. 24). One of the treasurers was the Rev. F. J. Faithfull, curate and then Rector of Hatfield and a J.P. A board announcing the scale of awards hung in the Market House.

In 1809 the minutes record: ordered that the Sum Five Guineas be given to Daniel Gray and John Gamkin for their great Exertions in tracing and being the means of Apprehending of Field and Glassbrook now in Hertford Gaol on suspicion of stealing an Ass from Daniel Gray and of breaking into the house of John Gamkin and stealing thereout sundry articles of Wearing Apparel. Field and Glassbrook were transported to Australia, but in 1812 Henry Glazebrook was prosecuted for returning before the end of his sentence of transportation!

Most of the rewards were for information concerning the theft of straw, wood, corn, potatoes and (once) sugar—all necessities of food or warmth, reminding us of the desperate plight of the poor. Later the character of law breaking seems to have changed to horse and sheep stealing, but in 1820 there was a wave of lead stealing, Brocket Hall and Lemsford Mill being singled out for special attention.

In 1839 a questionnaire was circulated to all Justices of the Peace asking about the state of crime in their own districts, what provision if any was made to deal with it and if they thought a local police force would be of use. Sir Robert Peel had established the Metropolitan Police in 1829, and it was felt that the same system might be extended to rural areas. Two returns for Hatfield were made, by Rev. F. J. Faithfull J.P. and the 2nd Marquess of Salisbury, J.P. The Rector stated that there was of course plenty of crime, mostly wood and turnip stealing, and no way of dealing with it, he could not say if a rural police force would help. The Marquess said there was a lot of wood and turnip stealing, usually not worth the trouble of prosecuting, that "A Beadle acts as watchman and Constable, receives 6s. a week from the Churchwardens, 10 shillings a week from private subscription"—this may refer to the activities of the Association mentioned above. But the Marquess added a note: "As long as the Police of London and that of other large towns neglect to search the carts of suspicious persons at their entrance into their district, the establishment of a rural police is perfectly nugatory".

The County Police Force

The County Police Act of 1839 authorised the Justices to set up a full time police force for a county, or a division of a county, to be paid out of the general county rate, though until the 1914 war they were paid and regarded as unskilled labourers. Hertfordshire adopted the Act in 1840 and in 1841 the first Chief Constable, Captain Archibald Robertson of Kincardineshire, Scotland, was appointed, and held office up to the time of his death in 1880 at the age of 75.

When Mr. Robertson took charge of the force, the county was organised into ten divisions (there are now six). He had under him four Superintendents, six Inspectors and sixty Constables (no sergeants). The estimated annual cost was £5,200.

Membership of the County Police Force required few qualifications in those days, but they had to be men of intelligence and strong character. They were not noted for their physique, however, as the average height was 5ft. 7¾ ins., some being as short as 5ft. 6ins. and very few over 6ft. tall. The first uniform was top hats and frock coats (see Fig. 5) which was changed in 1891 to helmets and tunics.

Fig. 5. Hatfield Police outside their Station at Goldings, French Horn Lane. Believed to be about 1880. From a photograph belonging to the late Miss Hicks.

In the Hertford Mercury of Jan. 1845 we find a report of the Police Committee's quarterly returns. "The number of persons who have been apprehended or summoned during the quarter amounted in all to 511, of whom 374 have been convicted and punished or sent for trial. During the last six months 7 sheep were stolen from the Rural Police District. There are upwards of 225,000 sheep kept. In the corresponding months of 1843, 34 were stolen; 1841, 62 stolen; 1840, 160 stolen. This last period was prior to the introduction of the Rural Police Force in the county. Within the last 6 months, 6 men have been transported for sheep stealing. Amount of property reported stolen during the quarter, £116 13s."

The Chairman of Quarter Sessions (Lord Salisbury) objected to the report about sheep stealing, which he said was "got up for the purpose of placing the *Police* in a favourable light. He had before protested against such statements being sent to the Court, and he must remark that they were calculated to provoke opposition to the Police; and if that force were to go on quietly it must not be in this way. He must say himself that the force was a most *inefficient* one; of the cases that had come before him not one in ten had been discovered by the Police, and the only thing they had done in his neighbourhood (Hatfield) was to find an obsolete Act of Parliament by means of which they tormented some

23

unfortunate individuals for selling squibs. He protested against the reception of the statements to which he had referred. When he was decidedly of the opinion that the force was not efficient, he could not be expected to say it was efficient by giving his sanction to such statements as were introduced with the report".

Following this, the editorial of Jan. 11th, 1845, reads: "We have inserted in another column a letter from a valued correspondent (signed 'C') in reference to the remarks made by the Marquis of Salisbury at the last Quarter Sessions, on the inefficiency of the Police Force in the county. The fair and reasonable manner in which the writer treats the subject releases us from the necessity of making any lengthy reference to it. We may, however, remark that H.M. Judges seem to have arrived at very different conclusions to the Chairman of the Quarter Sessions, in proof of which we may state that at the last Assizes, Baron Gurney ordered rewards to be given to five members of the County Police for their efficiency in detecting offenders. When a Judge feels himself authorised thus to distinguish men whose ordinary duty it is to detect thieves, it is but reasonable to suppose that he must have formed a very high opinion of their efficiency and zeal.

We trust that the remarks of Lord Salisbury were made hastily. If so, it would not ill become his Lordship's character and station to reconsider the opinion he has pronounced, and if possible to lend his influence to make the Force more efficient than it really is, rather than to supply disaffected and unreasoning persons with the materials for an injurious agitation, which cannot fail to lessen the efficiency of the Rural Force, just to such an extent as it may succeed in withdrawing from them the confidence of any portion of the public."

The first Police Superintendent of Hatfield was Isaac Pye, appointed on 14th May 1842. In 1851 the police force in Hatfield consisted of an Inspector, Abraham English, who was an Irishman and lived at the police station in Ivy Cottage next to the Gun in Newtown; two constables, Joseph Wilson living in Park Street and Charles Randall in Fore Street, and a third constable at Newgate Street called William Ryder. The name Charles Randall is of interest, since a Hatfield man of exactly the same name who joined the force in 1911 rose to become Deputy Chief Constable, retiring in 1937. We do not know if there was any relationship.

In 1881 under the new Chief Constable, it was decreed that every sergeant and constable should attend church at least once every Sunday wearing uniform, and this order was carried out by the recruits training at Hatfield until as recently as 1938.

The Force was gradually increased throughout Hertfordshire, and in 1881 was reorganised into five Divisions. In 1899 the strength was 197, and more duties fell within its scope, especially with the advent of the motor car. The Local Government Act of 1888 which created the County Councils, put much of the administration of the Counties into their hands, but the County Police Force was put under the jurisdiction of a Standing Joint Committee of representatives of the Justices and the County Council, and so it remains.

About 1883 the headquarters of the County Police was transferred from Hertford to Hatfield, and the present buildings in St. Albans Road were put up. The Hatfield Police at this time had its Station at Goldings in French Horn Lane, now the headquarters of Holliers Dairy. (see Fig. 5). Hatfield was chosen as Police Headquarters principally because of its central position in the county, situated as it is on the Great North Road A.1. and a main railway line from London to the North.

The Force has kept abreast of modern developments. In 1947 a new system of two-way radio contact between Force Head Quarters and patrol cars, was inaugurated by the then Home Secretary, the Rt. Hon. J. Chuter Ede, M.P. Today these are commonplace, as too, are the patrol motor cycles, fitted with wireless equipment. Squads of young policemen training on these, with their L-plates, are sometimes to be

Fig. 6. Present day Police uniforms, showing a constable, a motor patrol officer, a policewoman and a cadet. The helmet was first adopted in 1891.
[*Photo: Herts Constabulary*

seen in the town. The Police Headquarters radio mast (see cover) is now a familiar land mark, and from Hatfield all the County's radio fitted patrol vehicles are controlled. The stables, formerly used by the horses of the mounted police, have been converted into garages.

The work of the Hertfordshire Constabulary was increased during the second world war through the practical administration of emergency regulations of the Home Office and Ministry of Home Security. These included the classification of aliens, organisation and supervision of an air-raid warning system, blackout enforcement and finding billets for evacuees. All this was added to their duties at a time when the younger members of the Force were leaving to join H.M. Forces.

In the early hours of 10th October 1944 a V.I. flying bomb fell at the rear of the headquarters at Hatfield, so badly damaging four police houses occupied by members of the staff that they had to be demolished, and wrecking part of the offices (see Fig. 7). About three hundred houses were damaged more or less severely in the same incident, and the police turned out to rescue and tend the people injured in these houses before attending to their own. Eight people were killed and twenty-six injured that night. The acting Chief Constable commended five members of the Force for their conduct on this occasion, and one received a commendation from King George VI in June 1945.

Fig. 7. Damage caused by VI flying bombs 10/10/1944. The photograph is taken from the direction of the old St. Audrey's School and the Petty Sessional Court appears in the background.

[*Photo: Herts Constabulary*

At the present time (1961) the Hertfordshire Constabulary stands at six Divisions commanded by a Chief Constable, with an Assistant Chief Constable, 858 men and 41 women on the strength. The Divisions are : (a) Bishops Stortford, (b) Hertford, including Hatfield, (c) Watford, (d) Hemel Hempstead, (e) Hitchin and (f) St. Albans. Each Division is administered by a Superintendent with Chief Inspectors, Inspectors, Sergeants, and Constables forming their full complement of police officers.

The first Policewomen in Hertfordshire were recruited in 1928, when two constables were stationed in Hatfield. Their duties were not confined to Hatfield but extended to all parts of the County. Normally, women officers work an 8-hour day with no night duty except on special occasions. Their work includes traffic and patrol duty, duty at Assizes or Quarter Sessions, child welfare, the investigation of all offences in which a female is concerned, assistance to the Criminal Investigation Department, and tracing missing women and girls.

There are three Departments at Headquarters: Administration, C.I.D., and Traffic. Administration Department deals with general administration, finance and accounting, recruiting, training and civil defence, uniform and equipment, and organisation. The C.I.D. is concerned with aliens, firearms, fingerprints, photography and criminal records. The Traffic Department deals with all Police vehicles, their garages and workshops, communications by radio, telephone and teleprinter, traffic accident statistics and road safety.

Fig. 8. The Petty Sessional Court House, Hatfield.
[*Photo*: *H. W. Gray*

27

We learn a lot about present day crime in Hatfield from the local weekly newspapers, and from the Magistrates' (Petty Sessional) Court which sits on Mondays in the Court House (see Fig. 8). The Juvenile Court also sits there. Minor offences are dealt with summarily, and the more serious ones are heard at Hertford or St. Albans Quarter Sessions before a jury.

There are at present fifteen Justices of the Peace (Magistrates) in the Hatfield Petty Sessional Division, which includes the parishes of Hatfield, North Mimms, and Northaw, the chairman being Sir Geoffrey Church.

The incidence of law-breaking in Hatfield is about the same as for the country as a whole. The coming of the New Town has not so far made any appreciable difference, though there have been some cases of wanton damage to trees and verges, which we hope will cease as the new community settles down. The history of the town shows it has survived worse troubles in the past, and if its citizens become aware of that history they may feel new pride, and determination to make Hatfield a pleasant place in which to live.

NANCY BROWN

INDEX

31

William de Shuneshull 10
Wilson, Joseph 24
Wilson, William 15
Wisman, Robin 13
woodland 14

Woodside (Woodsyde) 7,
  20
wool trade 11
Workers' Educational
  Association 3, 29

World War II 26
Wright, Thomas 5
Wright, William 21

Y

Younge, Margaret 13

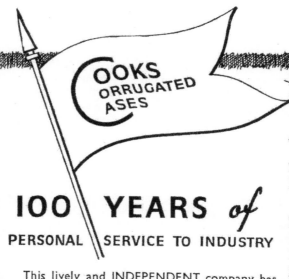